WHAT'S HAF
CAN BE FEL .

POETRY AND ART BY
MARTA BYER WHITE

BOOK DESIGN BY LYNNE BENTLEY-KEMP
PHOTOGRAPHY BY LYNNE BENTLEY-KEMP AND MARTIN WHITE

ISBN 13: 9781512388466
ISBN 10:1512388467
Marta Byer White©2015

Library of Congress cataloging-in-Publication Data

White, Marta Byer
What's Happening Here Can Be Felt By The Moon, 1st Edition

Additional photography by Brad Solomon

Cover image "Desire and Disaster" detail
back cover " The Deluge" detail, photos by Lynne Bentley-Kemp

To my twin sister Janet, whose own art reflects that beautiful soul and a life dedicated to it. Hand in hand we've gone through the voyage together.

Heartfelt thanks to Trish Hurley for her constant support and patience as my Executive Assistant over many years. You are my right hand and my heart.

To Martin. For fifty years, a shared life. He is the road taken. Quiet love behind many faces. Thank you for the beautiful photos of my artwork in this book.

What's Happening Here Can be Felt By the Moon

Third floor, Sloan Kettering Pediatric Cancer Ward
Dwarfs in a Greek tragedy, bald actors of courage
Swamp creatures breathing under water
Riding through cyan blue ice streams on Trojan horses
Dreaming of sledding down a snowy hill on new Flexible Flyers

Hasidic Jewish children with leukemia
Their souls already reaching toward darkness
Bracing themselves from an intruder
Who stands outside their hospital door
Secretly doomed, each day getting closer to oblivion

What's the missing link of Eastern European ancestry?
Who are the gatekeepers? The jury is out
Mothers rush to the armory to feed the frenzy
Wondering what is true and what is not yet discovered
"We don't know the question until we come closer to the answer
And if we don't know the answer, it's a religious question,"
The Doctors tell you, those corrupt whores

"A Greek Tragedy" mixed media box

I remember four year old Shimmy, my niece's youngest son,
Playing Doctor with his great-grandmother and a $10 toy set
Taking her temperature with a plastic stick in her drooling mouth
Wrapping a black bandage around a shriveled arm
Pressing its little red plastic pump to check her blood pressure
Sticks rubber tips into his ears
Listening to the beat of a caved-in chest
Big brown saucer eyes full of wonder
So serious about his medical mission

Young Shimmy, now dancing at his aunt's Hasidic wedding
A midget in a shiny lapeled suit
Tripping over his trousers
Meant to be worn for the next three years
A black adult hat held up by his big ears
Dancing on the shoulders of his eldest brother
Arms extended, clasping desperately with his outstretched hands
Who ha, who ha, stamp, stamp, joyously going round and round

Now at twelve, chemically tortured, swollen throat, burnt lips, a bloated body
A lethal act of violation, using him as an experiment
You suddenly realize it's the end of the book Life, a word
What's happening here can be felt by the moon

"Chemically tortured"
mixed media metal box

"We Don't Know the Answer"
paper collage

Unpacking the Boxes

Why didn't you give me your favorite things
When you were still alive?
Did you think you could take them to the grave
As in some Egyptian tomb
Or like Evita Peron into a mausoleum?

I continue to pack up the boxes
My favorite, an old Chinese man made of ivory
Going up a wooden path to nowhere
A hawk-like multi-colored bird in flight, porcelain
That blood red vase with gold flecks as rare as a black dahlia
An orange glass shaped like the Eiffel Tower

Remembering you caressing its divine details, your layers of truth
An eloquent meditation of time and memory
We feel time passing like a pulsating heart
Rushing past you, a kind of unholy wind
Sliding helplessly between what was and what is
Waving much of that era goodbye

"Bits and Pieces" mixed media construction

I still dream of those Buddha's everywhere in all positions
Made of jade, rose quartz, crystal, amethyst
All gone, sold to a greedy school principal
Bargaining, then complaining
"Do better, you're taking the food out of my children's mouths"
What's mostly left are Buddha's made of plaster, glass, terracotta
But still beautiful

My father, an invisible white star, elusive
Big little man, a paper tiger
Once said I was "the third leg, a leash around his neck"
Or was it "leech" sucking blood?
To this day I don't know
There were things I recognized
And a lot I missed
Why did you try to tear down one of your own,
We're cut from the same cloth
My face is yours

"What Was, What Is"   mixed media sculpture

Ashes to the Wind

In the holy city of Benares
    Monkeys sprinkled with red powder
    Run wildly through 5000 year old temples that took Three centuries,
    10,000 hands and 1000 deaths to build

Carved figures on buff pink veined stone
    With twisted ripe limbs, full nipples, hips and thighs Intertwined in
    lurid love positions
    As boats gently float by

A stream of shaven-headed priests in pumpkin orange gowns
    Sprinkle holy water as they pass,
    Pine nut prayer beads sway with their hypnotic chanting
    On the steps of a crumbling building, the elderly wait to die
    A young man carries the corpse of his son in a plastic basin
    Desperate to save the fetus
Places it at the feet of a holy man

"Ashes to the Wind" mixed media sculpture

Loved ones stoke fires under dead bodies
Tending to their task with meditative, dreamlike grace
Charcoaled bits of paper, ashes of twigs, burnt flesh
On my skin too, as though I walked through that same fire

Wailing widows, the scent of burning incense and loss
The squealing sounds of wild animals
As thousands bathe in the grey murky waters of the Ganges
Together with their sacred cows at dawn

A lone rowboat slips by a dead man without a friend to feed his fire
A turbaned hired hand in smoke stained rags, casting no shadow
Stands with a broken canoe paddle, his crutch, indifferent
Pushing what is left of the unloved body into the swollen river

Delicate thin layers drift off like pieces of yesterday's charred newspaper
In this city of sadness, temple bells toll in the distance
The funeral never ends, the burial never complete
Time a river, ashes to the wind

"Time a River"   mixed media box

"Temple Bells Tolling in the Distance"   mixed media box

Lust Never Sleeps

On a company trip to the city of Mosques
Golden minarets
Faded green pagodas with their filigree crowns
And seated elephants carved in blue marble
Surrounded by a fire hurricane,
Toxic chemicals surge, inky darkness
Pollution whipping and twisting in the air
He pays dollars for exquisite lessons
From a sex worker in Bangkok
Transformed by the touch of the Thai woman
Knees splayed and backs domed in submission
Solicitous souls that cut to the quick
Dancing girls wearing paper numbers
Clipped to bikini bottoms
Even female amputees and dwarfs
Lights spilling over child prostitute bodies
The whole skeleton illuminated by lust
Paying her to pleasure his business partners
As he watches, seems a natural thing to do
Wicked bastards, condemning little shits

With claim to virtuoso skills
This gang of blue chip dudes
The American corporate elite
With their tones of entitlement
Lies allowed to grow
"You have to protect yourself big time
Watch your money
They can give you change of ten instead of a hundred
These CEOs of Morgan Stanley and Jolly Roger
Hold court in Bangkok's best bars
Madison Avenue blowhards
One looks like Geraldo Rivera
In love with a Burlesque Queen, a dancer in this sex palace
Another like the fake blonde Lou Dobbs
With red capillaries on his nose and cheekbones
Wouldn't be caught dead in some museum tour
But does like a dog act that drinks alcohol, a cat that laughs,
and a vagina that smokes cigarettes and blows smoke rings
Nudging your ribs at every joke
"The next round of pussy's on me"

"Virtuoso skills"   Mixed media construction

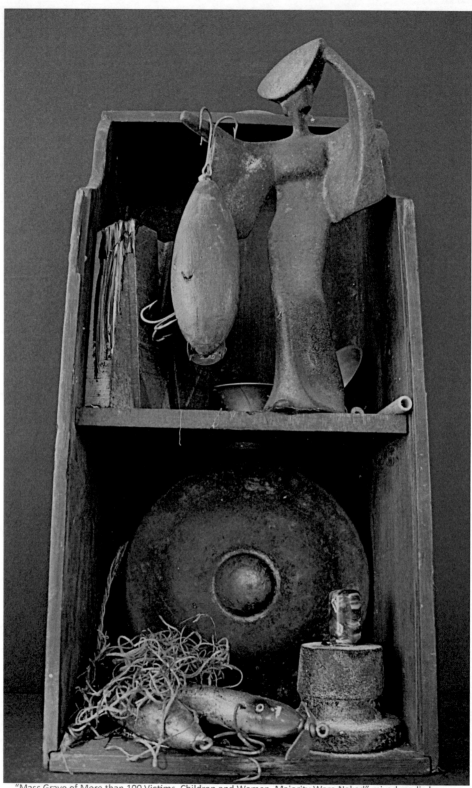

"Mass Grave of More than 100 Victims, Children and Women, Majority Were Naked" mixed media box

Rocks

In the flow of time
Rocks remind me of where I've been
And will never go back to
Pieces from my life, moments in time
The holy rocks of Benares
Picked from the muddy Ganges
The color of mussels, egg shells
As thousands lift up their golden saris
March their sacred cows into the swollen river
Filthy water at dawn flowing into the sea of oblivion
Pebbles covered with dung and red monkey powder
Reflecting back on decay
Before me, slivers found under a spreading deep-rooted 3000 year old tree
Growing under, next to carved stone temples
In praise of shadows, the ancient city of Angkor Wat
Shattered shards of the past frightening the birds
Under a deserted sky of colorless grey
I picked stones from a muddy field
Bloody garments popping through.
Where innocent Cambodians are buried, THE KILLING FIELDS
As a memorial, thrown into a glass tower fifty feet high
Skulls that have survived
Next to it, a shaky hand written sign
"MASS GRAVE OF MORE THAN 100 VICTIMS
CHILDREN AND WOMEN, MAJORITY WERE NAKED"

"In the Flow of Time" mixed media box

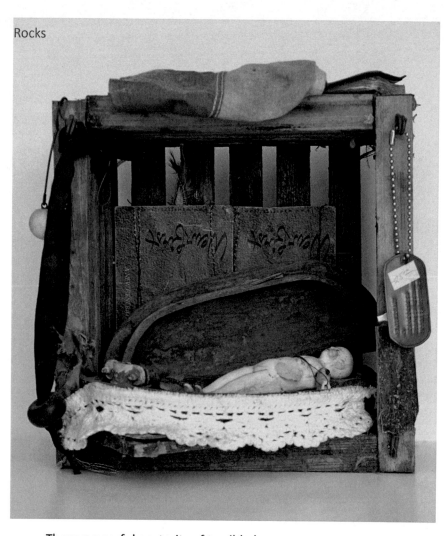

Those powerful portraits of terrible human cargo
Gorgeous soul sickness, still haunts me.
A Kafkaesque nightmare, a deafening sucking sound
That whole world covered in vaporizing ash
In my silence, I am screaming
Pol Pot, Pol Pot, Pol Pot
Cambodian Genocide.
One third of the population eliminated in just two years
Pictures of panic eyes looking straight at the camera holding its
faded number
Now those stones sit on my coffee table
In a wooden bowl, handmade from Senegal
Lest we forget

"Lest We Forget" mixed media box

"In My Silence I am Still Screaming"
mixed media construction

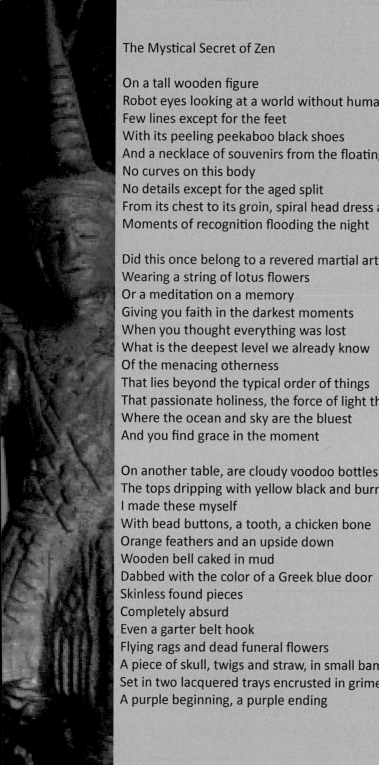

The Mystical Secret of Zen

On a tall wooden figure
Robot eyes looking at a world without humans
Few lines except for the feet
With its peeling peekaboo black shoes
And a necklace of souvenirs from the floating villages of Mekong Delta
No curves on this body
No details except for the aged split
From its chest to its groin, spiral head dress and wired arms
Moments of recognition flooding the night

Did this once belong to a revered martial arts master
Wearing a string of lotus flowers
Or a meditation on a memory
Giving you faith in the darkest moments
When you thought everything was lost
What is the deepest level we already know
Of the menacing otherness
That lies beyond the typical order of things
That passionate holiness, the force of light that touches the universe
Where the ocean and sky are the bluest
And you find grace in the moment

On another table, are cloudy voodoo bottles
The tops dripping with yellow black and burnt sienna paint
I made these myself
With bead buttons, a tooth, a chicken bone
Orange feathers and an upside down
Wooden bell caked in mud
Dabbed with the color of a Greek blue door
Skinless found pieces
Completely absurd
Even a garter belt hook
Flying rags and dead funeral flowers
A piece of skull, twigs and straw, in small bamboo holders
Set in two lacquered trays encrusted in grime
A purple beginning, a purple ending

"Finding Grace in the Moment" mixed media box (detail).

"A Purple Beginning" mixed media box(detail)

Bronx Park East

The father of the wealthy Kuntz family, neighbors next door
Was a wholesale butcher, a bit of a madman.
When he talked sounded like nuts being cracked
Clothes, an unmade bed.
His wife, a big mole on her face with hair coming out
Dye job of hazel color sewer water.
Looking like a girdle advertisement or a billboard
"Got Hemorrhoids? Say no to surgery."
 Had a ghost-like, deaf and dumb sleep-in maid
Their apartment, wooden Venetian blinds,dark green bindings
Pure silk gold lamp shades.
And the first black and white TV, a color gel over its face.
A Bronx storybook castle.

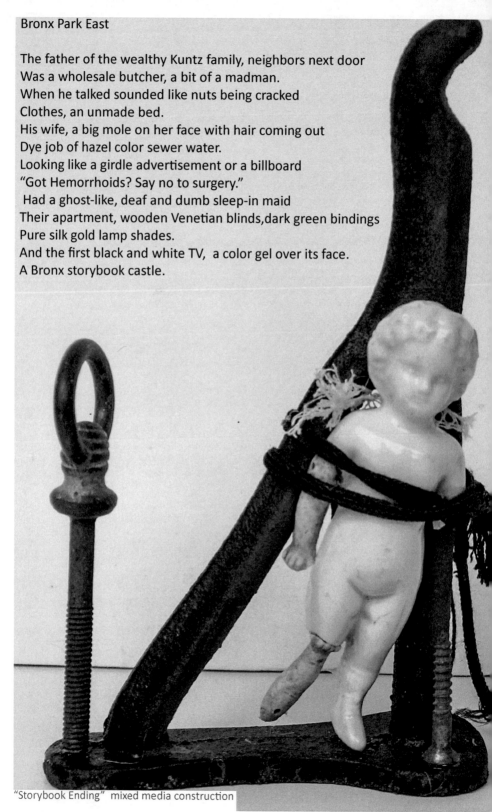

"Storybook Ending" mixed media construction

Vacationed at Florida's Beachcomber, a two story paradise
Drove there in a step-down Hudson, poodle cloth rug, a silver bullet to the moon.
The lobby, gold flocked wallpaper with a three-tiered Viennese Crystal chandelier
Reflecting the ornate mirror
Fat cherubs and rosettes on the side.
Cut-velvet upholstery furniture,
taupe ivory tassels on the bottom.

Mr. Kuntz, from Poland, used his Yiddish cup.
"Sewed three thousand dollars in the lining of his jacket
That's why he's so rich today."
His son had a Schwinn bicycle and
a Yankee Clipper sled.
Not some hand me down.
My age, a mongrel dog with angelic features
Forced me to dance in the gutter
Threw Sarsaparilla bottles at our feet.
"Dance, godammit, dance!"
He, the organ grinder. Us, monkeys.
Mr. Brave, snot coming out of his nose
Said "I can see from the back of my eyes
And eat soup with a knife."
Had enough allowance to buy twelve White Castle hamburgers
With ketchup, chopped onions
And a sliced pickle.
Sometimes gave us one "if we behaved."
Cold comfort.

"With Rosettes on the Side"
mixed media box

Our building had elevators like jailhouse gates
Hitting all buttons, alarms rang like a fire truck,
A screaming ambulance.
Buzz buzz for garbage on the pulley system.
Boiler room furnace blazing orange coal
Picture of hell, a Phoenix rising from the ashes.
The basement, our playground
Dark unfinished caves never ending
Filled with sticky spider webs, shadows on a grave
Cats and rats, silver garbage cans
The stench unbearable.
We'd crawl into secret places
No one ever found us.
The power, the high, was in the secret.

Terrible things happened there. Real cruelty.
Cats thrown in furnaces.
Strange men appearing from nowhere
We heard stories.
Once running in the cellar tunnel
A boy came toward me appearing from nowhere
Like a sword swallower or fire eater
White with features of a black person.
Trancelike state, fly open, fondled his thing down there
And me carrying a suitcase of fear
Ran into the elevator to save myself.
Told my father. Said "he's a goddamn putz. Not mean, stupid!
Has a deformed gene, the sense of a cow.
I'm gonna tell his mother.
The world is going down the fucking tubes!"

One day, a washing machine appeared
One for the whole building.
Signed up on the half hour, six am to midnight.
My mother, always late, screwed up the system.
But rooftops were still for drying, had rooftops then.
Each her own clothesline and a bag of wooden pegs
So clean laundry wouldn't fly like a kite through the back-
woods of the Bronx.

"Secret Places"
mixed media box (detail)

"Terrible Things Happened Here" mixed media box

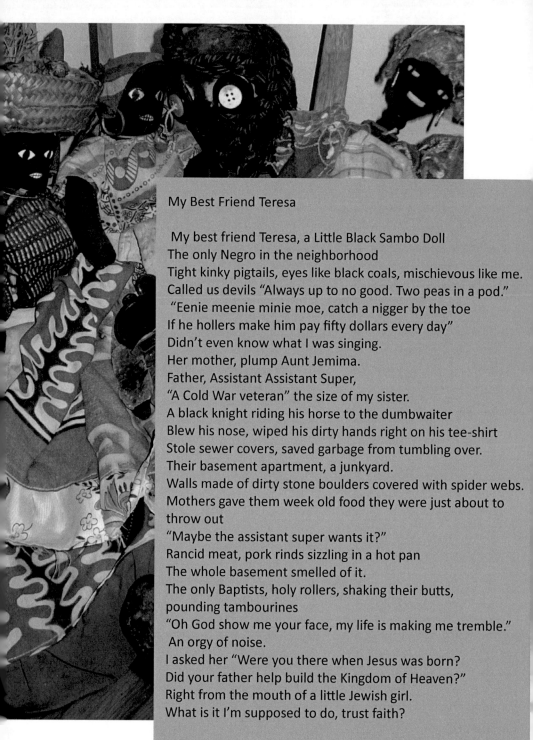

My Best Friend Teresa

My best friend Teresa, a Little Black Sambo Doll
The only Negro in the neighborhood
Tight kinky pigtails, eyes like black coals, mischievous like me.
Called us devils "Always up to no good. Two peas in a pod."
"Eenie meenie minie moe, catch a nigger by the toe
If he hollers make him pay fifty dollars every day"
Didn't even know what I was singing.
Her mother, plump Aunt Jemima.
Father, Assistant Assistant Super,
"A Cold War veteran" the size of my sister.
A black knight riding his horse to the dumbwaiter
Blew his nose, wiped his dirty hands right on his tee-shirt
Stole sewer covers, saved garbage from tumbling over.
Their basement apartment, a junkyard.
Walls made of dirty stone boulders covered with spider webs.
Mothers gave them week old food they were just about to
throw out
"Maybe the assistant super wants it?"
Rancid meat, pork rinds sizzling in a hot pan
The whole basement smelled of it.
The only Baptists, holy rollers, shaking their butts,
pounding tambourines
"Oh God show me your face, my life is making me tremble."
An orgy of noise.
I asked her "Were you there when Jesus was born?
Did your father help build the Kingdom of Heaven?"
Right from the mouth of a little Jewish girl.
What is it I'm supposed to do, trust faith?

"My Best Friend Teresa" mixed media construction

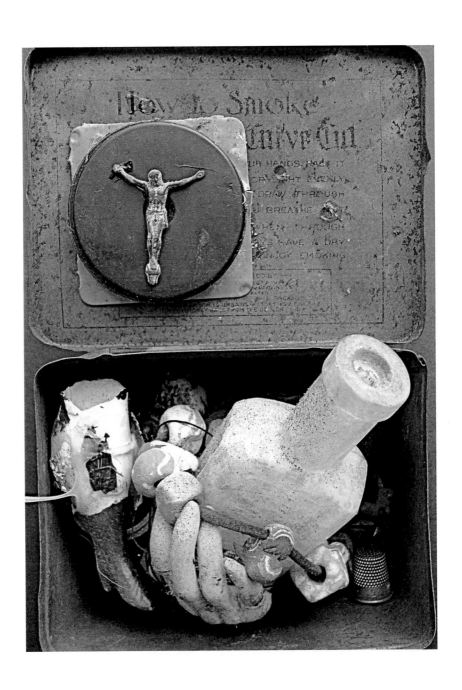

"The Kingdom of Heaven"   Tin box, mixed media

A Recent Widow

This woman named Peaches
Was the beauty parlor owner from Pelham Park-
way, Bronx
Her clumsy charm, like a burlesque flutter of fans
Having had a passionless marriage
"Sexually he was dull
Petty goals within the shadows of failure
And I was created to be the toy of a man, his rattle"
These forgotten bones are turning old
The ache of age seeps in my widow's joints
My past waves the present down
But I'm good enough. I'm smart enough
And gosh darn it, people like me!"
She learned this in her one and only AA meeting
After a night of heavy boozing

"Finally free, I wanna be a bird
It's beautiful to fly, blossom and roost
I always find men that cannot love
Still waiting for my prince
I want to be seduced *a la* Cinderella
Someone, please put a slipper on my foot
Believe me It's gonna fit. I'm ripe for an awakening
For the sheer thrill of it I want an operatic love story
You know, age is just a number
Sixty is the new forty
My husband was the first of the wannabe's
But as useless as a spun sugar snowflake
Died of Parkinson's, or was it Alzheimers?

I actually asked him, 'what do you want for
your last supper?'
I was serious, but he giggled"
Her voice hits your face
Like gravel thrown by a drunk who lost his
keys
Tight mouth like a row of stitches
Lips the color of a bloody wound
Wondering what she will do with the rest
of her life
The puzzle never stops
Ya know, I'm thinking of changing my name
to a planet
Whaddya think? Mars, Jupiter, Uranus?"

Now Peaches is having an affair with Yuri
The Allerton Avenue dry cleaning man
Wears the day glow orange cap she gave
him backwards
Makes him look like he might have sung
Nazi songs around the campfire
With a voice that sounds albino, he tells
her blue-eyed cats are always deaf.
I had Heinz Ketchup fights
with my ex old lady
It was spread all over the slippery kitchen
floor and the ceiling too
A disaster
A disarray of life.
"Faint joy must be paid for in equal
amounts of torment"

"I'm Ripe for an Awakening"
mixed media collage

The Kosher Chicken Store

As a child, twice weekly we'd go to the Kosher Chicken store
They had to be freshly killed
Sawdust on the bloody floor so you wouldn't slip or slide
The stench of hell as housewives made their pick
Feathers flew everywhere,
Running wildly, a red crescent moon perched on its head
Screaming plump birds
An orgy of noise, they knew their fate
Missing their barn homes, in front of windmills, salt lagoons,
Undulating pastures full of sheep
For a closer inspection, the butcher held them upside down
Like a baby encountering civilization for the first time
Slitting their throat, blood oozed everywhere
Dead, yet the body kept moving
Looking like an evil witch, my mother never satisfied
"Smells too scrawny, not enough meat on it
Don't like the white color, yellow is better
Don't forget to pluck off all its feathers until it's clean
We aren't here to make pretty things"
Out came the endless organs
"Save the liver, chop off the feet, we want them"
With their long toe-nails, chewy muscle alligator skin
Cooked over the gas flame, it was my favorite.
I knew I could never sew or glue the pieces together
Of that poor chicken
Once creatures of the earth
For them, God was far away

"Creatures of the Earth"
mixed media sculpture

24

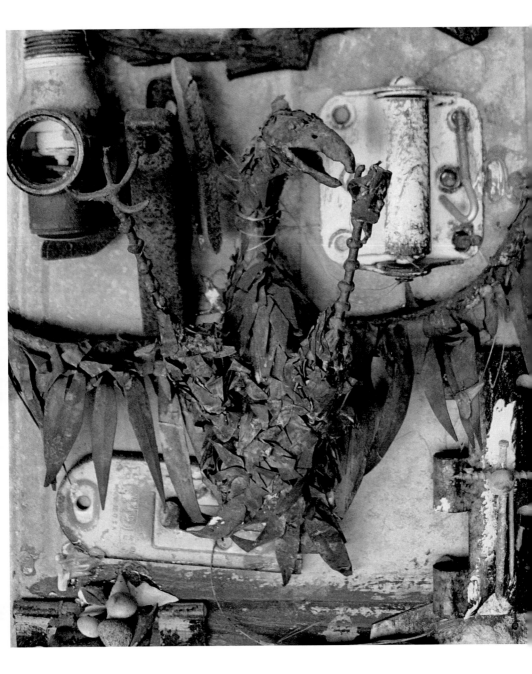

"For Them God Was Far Away"
mixed media construction

My Mother's Pocketbook

My mother's old pocketbook
Filled with lollipops covered in hair
Sticky candy, shredded tissues, a piece of old cookie
Marble Halva missing its silver cover
The coins also like they came from a garbage bag
With crusted nuts on cellophane paper
Always counting her change
A thirty-pound satchel of coins
Heavy as a Ft. Knox gold brick
This, the money she squirreled away
To have something in case my father left us
Afraid of the life she'll never live, a life that hasn't begun
When I needed 5 cents for milk and cookies at school
She lied, "I have no change, ask your father"
I widened my blue eyes without speaking
But I knew her hiding places and would just take it
Like a child's handprint left on a car window
It was under bloomers, stretched out bras, secret bank books
And glasses missing a lens. The brand: Helen Keller

"Tango With Cows" mixed media box (detail)

She once found condoms in my father's coat pocket
Does he go to massage parlors for sex
Trusting him less and less never knowing when he would return
When he did, this racehorse man with his movie star looks
Smoldering sensuality, his holiness himself
Was greeted with shrieks of air curdling disgust
Trees lashing out at each other, macabre foreplay
"Moving pawns back and forth!
You're a roamer, a strayer, a transient
We're split off and abandoned by you."

If he left, would I become a displaced person
Like the Jews in Krakow
Facing the firing squad past the point of no return
I often dreamed I found my mother's purse
With the hand of my father's woman friend she had murdered
The color, gangrene
Was it only a dog bone or a dead infant's hand?
The world, the reality we lived in, was invisible
In another dream, our alcoholic patriarch falls on a broken wine glass
Spilling into a map of abuse, love, loneliness
Sucking us into his impossible world
A tango with cows
I wished he'd vanish without a trace across the Straits of Oman
That place we learned about in school
Their ghosts are still at my door

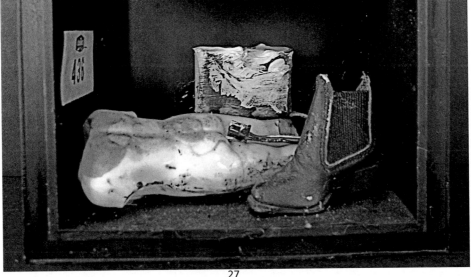

"Impossible World"   mixed media construction

"The Season of Cold is Eternal"
glass box, mixed media

In the Age of Deception

In the wrecking light
Watching the paint flake from the walls of
my room
Stuck in a hotel with generic tourists
In search of lost time
I walk amongst the very old
Like a widow toppling forward at the
grave, going in after myself
In a constant state of sickening dread
Signaling the apocalypse
In the Age of deception
Embracing the wind
The season of cold is eternal

Through the drawn curtains shines the
snow that I remember as a child
A skylark's egg in a bed of frost
The force of the light making a painted
white field
So different from when the ocean and sky
were the bluest
I'm in a migraine person's darkened room.
The death agony of a sacred cow
"You won't let me say what I needed to
say," shrieked the light
"And you are not here to bring me back to
bed."

Making love in bitterness
Lying in a grim embrace
Twisting with hate
He wakes in my body, broken like a gun
Bored after the massacre like the bour-
geois German elite
An ambitious wheeler dealer, this trickster
hero
White knuckled and sweaty
So cool and hip. One of the flash boys
Sounding like a sudden hiss of vegetables
in hot oil
When I try to speak my grief, all you hear
is a "high-pitched squeak."

29

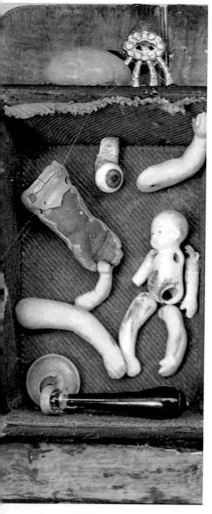

As I march deeper into the darkness
From the flames into deep shadow
My back now to the wall
Finally, sweet dreams
You invade my body

Frames of illusion
Sounds like the plucking of a lute string
Happy lovers going to the nuptial feast
But tenuous mellowness soon fades
What is obsolete now is the future
"Hold me. Hold me. Let me go!"
Or release me and restore me to the ground."
Blindfolded and hung from my shackled wrists
I am dead but my nails keep growing

Weaving in and out of sins and redemption
When he left, he left no stain of himself
Brutus, the ambitious.
Shriveled, flinching, this man of straw
Replacing love and trust with nothing. "Traitor!"
I can't even look into the face of flowers

Finding grace in the moment eludes me
"I'll be seeing you in all the old familiar places
In that small café and the park across the way
I'll be looking at the moon."
The stuff of old ballads.
Where does the truth of a life lie?
"All the roads that I walk will be away from you,"
Was the last thing I said to him.

"Sins and Redemption" mixed media box(detail)

A Path of Fire and Ice

Dreaming I'm in a jet plane
Suffocating, I can't breathe
High in the air
In a leaky vessel, shaking
Coming apart at the seams
Pressure in space and time
A zig-zag path of fire and ice
Doing all I can to hang on for dear life
I am utterly lost
Yet there's still a small burning light

Diagnosed with terminal melanoma of the G-spot
Cancer a fate as obscure as death by gas
I feel weighted down
By the sensation of drowning
Of being water boarded
Marooned on the far side of forever
Like a bullet as it travels through the barrel of a gun
Carcass crushed against the snow of a fucking glacier
Of smothering nightmares
A weariness that death rides on my shoulders
Suffering, chosen, unstoppable

The day I found out
The world smelled as it always smelled
Of newly cut grass, orchids and strawberry daiquiris
Perfumed people and bourgeois politeness covering
The suburban chaos with its jaded charm
A soft boiled wonderland
A yellow farewell summer

I saw a photograph of an old lady in an attic
And realized her face was mine
The science of our time has failed me
I cannot conquer it
I don't have a body
 I am a body

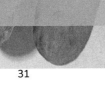

"A Yellow Farewell Summer"
mixed media construction

31

"I Don't Have a Body, I am A Body" mixed media box

"Last Wishes"   mixed media construction(detail)

Last Wishes

Through my morphine induced state
I tell him my last wishes
My old love listens

Don't bury me in some god-forsaken cemetery
Head stone to head stone
A house of cards, awaiting the domino effect
Instead, in my red lacquered coffee table
Deep and wooden with its heavy lid
The one exhumed from Phucket, Thailand
Then mark my grave with the sweet marble angel
The 400 year-old icon I shipped back from Chiang Mai

I want to be surrounded by pastures and cow herds
A warbler's song under a green lemon sky
Traces of an ancient summertime
While red-scarfed women go about their lives
Barns with beds of straw
A farm in the park, a petting zoo
With goats, sheep, rabbits
In a faux rural landscape of escape
Where children play
In patches of waist high summer grass
A corn maze to hide in
And people of all ages dancing the rhumba
Everything will sing

A River of Desire

The Grand Master
Impatiently waits for his dinner
His presence making me feel
I'm surrounded by a hive of bees
Pumped up by this awful frenzy
Is he bipolar? A manic-depressive?
A third rate student. A fourth rate college
Envious of the achievements of others
Dirties the pretty things

So I put my bourgeois magic to work
As curried goat boils like a sloshing sea
I chop and stir while daydreaming about utterly
rapturous sex
Mysterious, exciting, exhilarating
George Clooney kissing, caressing, reaching
Into the deeper recesses of our bodies
The best of me, the wild side
Wanting to become, once again
A river of desire

"A River of Desire" cut paper collage(above)

"A Shiver of Contact" mixed media construction

A shiver of contact. Shades of black
"What the hell are you cooking?
Smells like a buffalo herd
I wanted a bowl of soft boiled eggs
With runny yolks soaking into the bread
A blue plate special, not that exotic shit"
Acts as if a piece of meat flys through the air
With its guts coming out
A sense of deja vu
What is the thread that holds us together?

With his hair, done outrageously a la Donald
Trump
Tells me I treat him monstrously
His whole world depending on it
Like a timber awaiting a spark
This total debasement of my identity
Getting older and more cautious
At least you'd think he would get softer

"I Bow to the Inevitable"
mixed media construction

Caught with his pants down
I bow to the inevitable
I was trained to accept disappointments
But he is the elephant in the room
Ladies, let's all become lesbians
And live in a city of women
My favorite line in a play is
"Everyone has a 'we' except me
And not to have a 'we' makes you lonely"

He Knew His Fate

In the corner of my kitchen
Eyes fall on two pictures
The first, a tortured young face
My Mother's favorite brother Max, drowned at six
I am his namesake
His frayed picture with its haunting eyes
Mouth open as if to scream
He knew his fate
The second, me swimming at six
In that cold lake
My Mom fearful of chills, blue lips, Polio
Images of an iron lung with your head sticking out
Of a silver rocket to the moon
Sister Kenny,March of Dimes
And a brave poster child
With a brace on her withered leg
Next to smiling FDR on a wheelchair throne
Unblinking, looking up at the sun-lit sky
Now it's waiting for the big C
Ovarian, Uterine, Breast, red capsules up
Chemo or bone marrow
With glistening IV bags of Sodium Chloride, Paxol,
Platinum, Cytoxan, like hanging clouds
Take your pick

"He Knew His Fate"
mixed media box

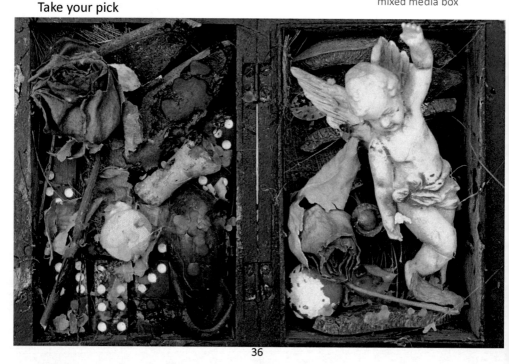

36

"I Am His Namesake"
mixed media construction

"We Were Falling So Fast"
mixed media box

"Never Enough Room" mixed media box

Love is Dark Work

In that season of deep mistrust
Sky overcast with a hint of Titian pink
The color of oil slicked water
Recovering from a hangover
Or drinking his way into one
Mr. Cactus Flesh stomps in again
Fierce and insistent
Looking like a wanted criminal
Disclosing then withholding
His presence verges on the dutiful
Even sees doing laundry as an emotional
commitment
Half wanderer-in, half wanderer-out
Bringing in waves of resentment

Doesn't resentment lose its novelty after
a while?
"I want someone neat and gentle
A soft voice who trusts me
Not someone who writes fake sex letters
to Penthouse Forum and is an aficionado
of the former Screw magazine
Love is dark work
You have to get your hands dirty"
But we were falling so fast
The engine just quit

38

And me, walking on my toes until they bleed
Without a clue as to how I used to not be
With the illusion of a future
This control freak keeps leaving me every time I get
used to him
The tension between irony and sincerity
Brutalizing each other like wrinkled spoiled children
There's never enough room in the house for both of us
I wish I could walk away from this one without regrets
Perhaps the fault is in our stars

"Desire and Disaster"
mixed media box

My Mother's Last Hour

On a steel blue afternoon
The ground is covered
With shriveled blossoms and bitter little apples
Birds sing the wrong tunes in the wrong trees
Too early in the season
Bleating for their mothers
They wait and wait
Not yet knowing how the world works
Oddly poignant
Remembering now my mother's last hours
Her arms discolored blue and gold rainbows
From blood clots, needle pricks
Her breath, a crackling shell into bleak water
Frail body shivers, gurgling her last meal
Not the Chinese food she loves
But the acidic food from that nursing home
Beyond the knife
The right side paralyzed she pulls with her other arm,
white knuckled and sweaty
Tries to rip off clothes on the skin of her mummified body
Stretching her withered arms and shriveled feet
A lonely spasm of helpless agony
Her soul already in that dark place
An earthy hell
Until the morphine takes hold
And she moves toward the primrose path
Meandering through gardens of forgotten pasts
Floating memories, ghosts on a throne
Madness in the spring
Passes to the other side
South of heaven beyond betrayal
The endless dress rehearsal is over
Her chin lifting, smiling angelically
Skin radiantly clear lids close so peacefully
All lines disappear from what had once been her face
"Forgive me, Forgive me," were the last words she spoke
Did she miss her destiny?
Her soul, a sacred language, is now being born in me
It's strange to give up a mother's love
The season of cold is eternal.

"My Mother's Last Hour"
mixed media box (detail)

"Faraway Nearby"
mixed media sculpture

Aunt Gertrude

In a Jewish home for the aged
Outside Riverdale New York
Aunt Gertrude sits
In a fog of Alzheimer's
One foot dangles in mid-air like a puppet with a broken string
Her teeth in a glass,
Food morsels floating to the top
Mouth opened as if in a scream
The only thing moving, a snakelike milky white tongue
In a black hole of a drooling mouth
I stroke her purple veined hands
Gold, black and blue from pushed needles.
Soothingly I say, let go, just let go until you disappear
Like a ray of light on the inside of someone's eyelid,
A meditation, a flash of something
Until you slowly drift to the other side
Howling in fear.
Twisted summer sleep
No one knows the moment God chooses
No one knows the time, the clink of the closed coffin
How many mornings remain?

I arranged for a private companion
No more screaming "nurse, nurse, I need you nurse" down an empty hallway
And no one comes
The Russian woman speaks Yiddish to her
"Are you a relative?" my aunt asks
Smoothing her bloodless skin
Cheerful warm, a paid gigolo
Easing her into the freshly dug hole
Until she fills that empty grave
The far-away nearby

"Another Fall From Grace"
mixed media construction

Another Night in Suck City

Peddling his bike on Detroit's deserted streets
A drunk, small and gritty
Lies bruised after a crack bender.
With his bleak hollow face
And watery jellyfish eyes
Has another fall from grace.
Sees everything in slow motion
The secret history beneath the streets
Even pictures of roller skating horses.
Imagines he's confronted at every corner
By raggedy unshaven little men
Sustaining themselves on cabbage

The air howls and sobs with laughter
"You will be wet" shrieks the wind to
Those way, way back failed ones
Infused with nostalgia
They sit on benches in a battered water park.
An elderly organ player
Shakes his paper cup for handouts
Another tells jokes for pennies
"Forget about the other thing Mrs. Lincoln
How was the play?"
Then adds, "never say die"

Illusions shattered, this stink hole of old age
Live in the shadows
Surrounded by neighborhood gangs
Bloods, Counts, Crips, Guardian Angels
All could die from a zip gun, a stray bullet, overdosing,
The next crash
Urinating in each others mouths for fun.
Around the corner
A gang leader lies spread-eagle
Jesus Christ dead on the gutter floor
His body, like theirs, fragility and desires
Becomes a peaceful sense of nothingness
A disarray of life
Their future has been stolen.
On to nameless, Potter's Field

"A Peaceful Sense of Nothingness"
mixed media box (detail)

"A Long Way Gone" mixed
media construction

Online

In the Wild Horse Press
Rape is viewed as titillation
Guns, knives, weapons stuffed into various parts of the anatomy for the
sheer thrill value
Even portraying murder as a sexual turn on
Stallions choking in erotic rapture, spilling into fantasies of submission
Substance abuse, suicide attempts
Hiking in the nude, finding yourself in a blind alley thinking you're boiling
to death
That changing mirror in which you watch yourself disintegrate
Pretending to be Ludwig of Bavaria
Until you disappear into the fog with three transvestites
Before a neon sign saying "Stop"

Addiction tailspins, a long way gone
Losing the capacity for embarrassment
As you drink vodka out of a baby bottle in the shower
Wearing an organdy Indian scarf, a crying Buddha
Covering yourself in a tattered mink bedspread,
A gift from a friend dying of Aids
Imagining you're making a movie about your own life.

The tipping point, the power of habit
Looking for that drug-induced state of calm
Where everything sings
Zero day, you have chosen
Dying from a heroin overdose in a blacked out filthy room
In this white city, a sacrificial loser lured back by the devil
The hidden powers of the mind reinvent the next Marquis de Sade

"The Kingdom of Heaven" (detail) mixed media box

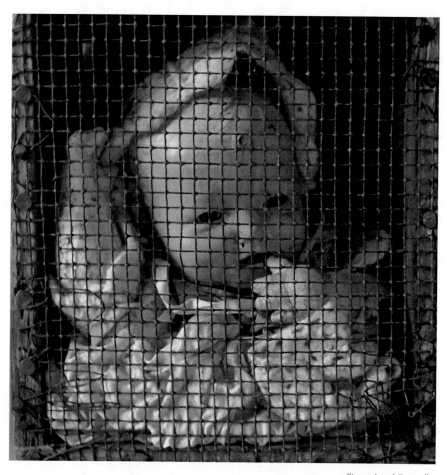

"Imagined Faces"
mixed media box

The Missing Is On Her Lips

In the wilderness of the city
A dark alleyway, claws of light
As rain pours down in sheets
Under what used to be called a moon
I see someone's daughter
Laid out on the ground washed in rainwater
Spread-eagle over piled garbage
Wearing cargo pants and a toe ring
A red ant colony crawling all over her body
Shoeless, feet covered in muck
A storm cloud of hair
Skinny as a rod with tiny breasts
Arms draped in cheap Indian jewelry
Still holding a bouquet of sweet peas
A gift for mother's day

"The Best And Worst of Myself"
mixed media construction

Hash in a plastic bag, old lipstick, chamomile tea
Photographs of cats spill out of her tattered drawstring bag
Through glazed eyes, close-up at a distance
Clouds shift, stack and move on
Rooms in pictures, rooms in dreams
Steam trains, dream trains
Travelling without a map, dreaming of her own life
Illusion in motion
Sees behind imagined faces
Relationships dissolving before they begin
The missing is on her lips
Creepily captivated, I move closer and see
That young girl is my daughter
The best and worst parts of myself
Covering her with a blanket made of a hundred pairs of Debutante's lace gloves
I was counting on her to be the dutiful daughter
Standing vigil at my deathbed
I can only bear to see her through a key hole
Is this a dream?

"Standing Vigil"
mixed media construction

A Bleak Bloody World

Caught in a rash of brambles
Under a sunken barbecue snagged with
thorny roses
I dreamt my father was weeping
I cannot help him, he is dead
In his hand a skylark's egg on a bed of frost
Lying next to a decomposing dead sheep
And a cat's last hour before dying of AIDS
Walking on spongy, bloody grass, my boots are
soaking wet.
My father's shame, his daughters blame
From him no light shines back at me
Just visceral glacial ice
His slow motion collapse, unstoppable
Past the point of no return
And me waiting for the next crash
An out of control runaway train

The untold story, a false glimmer
Flush times and fever dreams
We live in a magic hall of mirrors
Illuminations mixed with melancholy.
In this house of cards, shallow vulgarity,
Goosed-up intrigue
I plead for anonymity.
Secrets and truths. Bravado and bluster.
A deep dark conspiracy in his heart.
The smokescreen, a relentless hurtful squeeze
The way a cheetah pursues a sickly gazelle
As life shifts, he's a ghost in the sunlight
Calls me "daughter of the morning star."
His voice, the sudden hiss of vegetables in hot oil
Inventing passion and deceit.

Top: "A Father's Shame"
cut paper collage

Bottom: "Daughter's Blame"
cut paper collage

We fight furiously
An ancient ritual we have to undergo.
Returning at night as a stranger to this city of Scheherazade
Yet we still play children's games
"Ring around a rosy pocket full of posies, ashes, ashes, all fall down."
With his sexual innuendos, I'm nagged and undermined.
"Your tits are sticking out."
Answering "You treat me like a stripper who shoots up Viagra
In a room full of truckers gone wild
A woman who trades sex for powdered cocaine.
And you, you're a peeping Tom walking the streets by night
Surrounded by strip clubs and Daiquiri bars that are playing Bon Jovi songs
Your song, that of the shark, the paper snake."
I sit motionless against the winter shining
Being an old maid is like death by drowning
"If you don't get married soon you're gonna die on the vine."
Answers "then why the hell is it that I am still here with you?"

"Death By Drowning" mixed media box (detail)

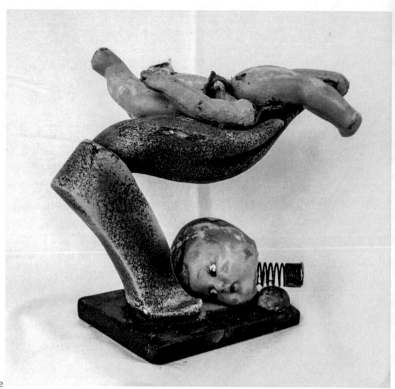

"Shared Solitude"
mixed media sculpture

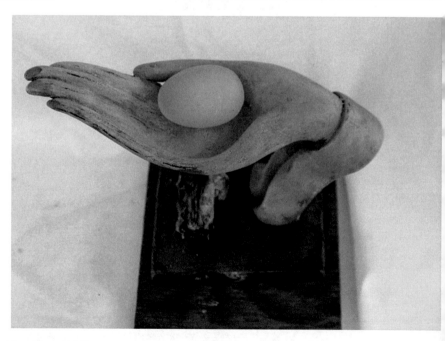

"Love Takes A Long Time to Die"
mixed media sculpture

Love Takes a Long Time to Die

I knew I was in love
When I thought it was over
And had the image of a mile long umbilical cord, cut
Lying shriveled and bloody at my feet
I knew I was in love, when he left
And it felt like a shotgun
Blasted my stomach away
Feeling I had nothing, I am nothing, I want to die
The more he ignored me
The more I loved him
I'm at the bottom of an empty jar
Love takes a long time to die

In the stillness accordion notes come from a distant player
Choirs of angels sing in unison
Playing the Wedding March
I'm still looking for a path to redemption
Or a nomadic way of life, alone
Not this shared solitude
Just let me walk away
Love takes a long time to die

" At The Bottom of an Empty Jar"
mixed media box (detail)

"A Gorgeous Chaos"   mixed media box (detail)

The Five and Dime

Just past the lubrication bay of the local garage
Is Woolworth's Five and Dime, the store that has everything.
Going down the aisle, delicious messiness, chaotic serendipity
Hairnets like spider webs, silver curling irons that could sizzle your hair
Nestle's hair dye capsules in every color
Paper cutouts "my girl is going to the office. mine to the prom
With a rhinestone crown and silver wand so she won't look loveless"
And the superhero comic books, after reading, would sell them
Three cents with cover, two cents without.
My aunt Gussie would buy Vick's Vapor Rub
The jar, Antarctic blue like broken edges of the sky or a seaside destination
Rock crystal candy on a string, rough diamond shape
That you would suck for sore throats
And God-awful cod liver oil, the color of yellow jack bees
Recommend by Carlton Fredericks, a radio health guru
Smelled like rotten fish even when the top was on.
But most important, a red rubber enema bag
Used for every kind of childhood sickness
It would hang over the bathtub on a shower curtain rod
My mother wouldn't close the silver hook
Until you screamed "I can't take it anymore!"

Going down another aisle, psychedelic Yoyo's
A fireball that takes your troubles to the moon
Garter belts, the elastic X crossing your stomach
Girdles, with laces as high as a grandma's shoe
And beautiful Crayolas I would grate for my miniature tea set
Altering the colors of my mind
"You're not my friend if you don't eat it."
Most special, a two-drawer pencil set
Covered with fabric flowers I had never seen before
A real eraser, a silver pencil sharpener
And magic cardboard games of illusion, all for ninety-nine cents
A perfect birthday gift you had already played with
Only the cellophane torn
And Pin the tail on the Donkey with a real poison dart inside
Or the turning Kaleidoscope with patterns magically changing
A trickle view of moths, after they spawn and die
Making the world an exquisite Universe
Minute Man silos, model slave ships, airplanes
Put together with mysterious honeycomb glue
A machine gun that's really a lunch box for boys only
Once for Christmas I was given a loneliness doll
Wearing a lime green ruffled taffeta dress made me feel I could be somebody else
Of course we never had money to buy this gorgeous chaos
The indignities of middle class
Reality, a stage set

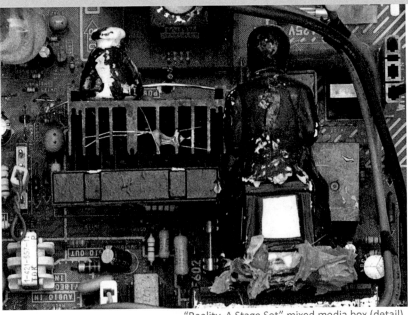

"Reality, A Stage Set" mixed media box (detail)

"Homage to My Sister" mixed media construction

I. Dreary Domesticity

My mother had the power of Faye Dunaway
Raging with a wire hanger
Was demoted from Courtesan to Housekeeper
Think or swim, her battle cry
Said I was on the other side of why
That bucolic little home produced a Jesus freak
A drug addict and an erotic fag, me
Our household broke apart, collapsed in muted increments
Like an exhausted horse falling in slow motion
"Cat ate the parrot, dog ate the cat"
I buried her nude in an unmarked grave
She had deflowered me
"When I sleep, I see behind every curtain
Lap dancers and whores, drag and muscle queens
The shape of my desires like a Diva workshop
The new queer of the lust generation
I have walls and walls of valentine candy boxes from ex-lovers
At a certain age, Happy Birthday is a victory song"

Absurdity bubbles up, a bruising passion saves oneself from loneliness and loss
You're more gone that way
Did you know that rats licked and groomed grow up braver and bolder
Thanks to the generous tongues of their mothers

And if you're asking........... I like fragrant ripe apples and runny eggs
Salt-rimmed Margaritas, Harvey Wallbangers and cock fights
My fantasy, nasty little sex with strangers
I'm a stuffed toy, a pacifier
Created to be the toy of a rich man, his rattle
Even though I came from egg shells,
I'm a high bred Persian cat, all cashmere fur
A butterfly person, part of the gay rat pack
A rock in the middle of an ocean,
A serpent with its tail in its mouth
I was born this way

"I Was Born This Way" cut paper collage

II. Under My Glass Ceiling Dumbo Duplex

Close up at a distance
Against the blackness of space
I hold court
I can tell you tales of madness and lurid love affairs
Zorro, my gretest
A natural born sex waif, that queer in camouflage
Could even fool Houdini

Our lovers' discourse and almost manic candor
Merciless, penetrating like captive animals
Contemplating a return to nature
Caught in a exhausting game of mirrors
Always threatening to take his life
Drano, a phone cord, a swan dive from a cliff
We had a pact
If one of us died, the other would too

Winter time in the Hamptons
He walked straight into the crashing waves of the sea
Wearing a wedding gown, long lace gloves
A veil with a tiara
Even a wrist corsage and a rope of cultured pearls
Down to his bellybutton
His body, finally discovered
Washed up on the sands
Covered in seaweed, slivers of glass, fish bones
Bulging eyes, bloated lips, decomposing flesh
Sequined slippers still tied on
An ashen lunar landscape
Darkness meets darkness
Supper for crows and seagulls
Heaven township

"Close up at a Distance" mixed media construction

"Heaven Township" mixed media construction

'Remembering Last Night"   ceramic, mixed media

Remembering last night

A fluid sense of truth comes over me
He, talking to a blond wig in a long purple dress
Cut down past her tits
A gorgeous hussy smelling of Tea-rose oil or is it Tabu
Accusing her of giving him blue balls.
This abiding attraction can easily turn into revulsion, obsession
The power is the promise of what's between her legs
Wolves don't kill nice, Tigers will kill you first
But wolves just rip you open and eat your guts alive
He wants to know how much I'm willing to bleed for him
That tearing down of an empty room
Delirium of daily life?
The impossibility of passion coexisting with rationality
One morning you wake up realizing
He can stray then beg for forgiveness
Banging on a shut door to be let back inside
The power is in the refusal
Living isn't about success
It's about fucking compromise

Burning the days from the moon's black side
Shaking at the sound of a twig snapping
My vitality dims like a diamond slave in a dark, dark tunnel
Memory, repetition, appearance, forgiveness
I am that rare window
Peeking into a hidden world
Wanting an ice ax to break the sea frozen inside me
Listening to the earth laughing at me
As if new dreams were ever possible

We are just a bunch of doomed people going nowhere
And each second of every day getting closer to oblivion
The end, dying alone in a nursing home built for holocaust survivors
"Margaret Teits, Flushing NY"
The ugliest sounds I ever heard
In a crowded hallway, a lineup of wheelchairs
A foghorn voice calling
And nobody comes
After my death I will fade quickly into obscurity
And who am I?
I am no one

"Peeking Into A Hidden World" mixed media box
(detail)

"The Ugliest Sound I Ever Heard" mixed media collage
(detail)

"Who Am I ?" paper collage (detail)

"The Great Pretender"
mixed media construction

The Great Pretender

His cracked leather address book of teenage mistresses
Lies spread open, embalmed on the bathroom floor
An open grave
Disgorging the bile of his hypnotic sexual obsessions
He's as greedy as a pig
Walking into his room I feel waves of resentment
Those empty summer nights pumped up by his frenzy
He mourns the approaching loss of his own mortality.
A descendant of a clown full of fabrication
An undercover agent spying, a master of disguises
This humorless man in an overly worn blazer
Thinks Brooklyn is the new Upper East Side
Our romantic life has become a real estate situation.

Who am I? A sinking hole of old age
Branches torn away into an unsafe life
My impulses on hold, head floating to the ceiling
Face, an ash colored mask, heavy breathing beneath it
Wandering around the wreckage of my domestic life.
Limping obese me on the verge of emotional collapse
Wanting to become once again an object of desire.
I want to leave the land of toxic waste
Into a world that is sunny, warm and clean
Spring comes with house sparrows on my windowsill

opposite page

"A Master of Disguise"
paper collage

63

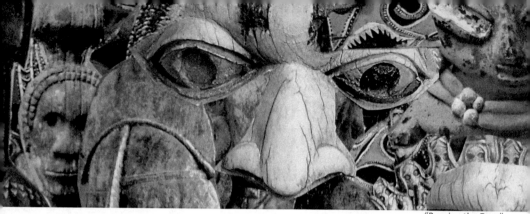

Phone Sex

Burning the days
Bored with the noise of everyday life
She chats the guy she recently met on Facebook
"I know it's 4 AM but I woke up lonely
I'm Sparkle, a bossy Contessa, queen of the night
A sex Goddess with a femine fatal flair
The one with the house full of Mickey Mouse memorabilia
And props from Star Wars, a UFO cultist who's fragrant and over ripe, remember?
I still live in discos, but now secretly taking pole dancing lessons,
Still dreaming of being a Go-Go dancer on a plexiglass table top
Go to my Facebook page, see my picture
I look like a Natural Born Sex Waif,
Anyway, told you I love men's chest hairs
My belly still tickles from last night's dude.
My bed is surrounded by gold-leaf mirrors, cherubs on the sides,
I'm blind to consequences
The portrait inside my head is that you're a woman's man
A major doma in for the long haul with a cult following
A ghoulish kitschy flair for rough sex"

Puffing a cigarette, in a hoarse voice, he says
"You just interrupted my fucking nightmare
Dreamt I was freezing to death in the Antarctic night air
Only to find when day broke, I stumbled onto
The Sahara Desert where I would die of heat.
But I'll give you a few meager clues
I'm now seeing cosmos of light over the cool city, red shells of firecrackers
My skin is on fire, fast, dense like dark ice
I can slide, thrust, jam and sink like an iron bar into water

Hypnotic sex brings me to the edge of the world
Burying secrets that lie beyond the typical order of things
You know, there's always a primal struggle for power, strong over weak
The scoundrel's seduction: conquer, enslave, then erase
Yet I'm still a creature of habit and routine
But this pre-dawn dark never learned to lie
If you want me, here I am, you can have me"

In her low voice, "I too am part of the lust generation
Tired of longing, missing, relenting, regretting
Living a centerless life, a spoiled Eden.
Reaching a dead end, makes me smaller and smaller
My screaming voice says 'I'm ready for the day of the locust'
The truth, I'm a ex-ex-ex-hooker with a perm dye job
Between pomegranate and pimento red
Now I make bikini bottoms and sew men's ties for a living
But I still hear summertime sounds and the Hollywood Dream Machine
And want a second chance
This time I'll be as faithful as lassie... your sex slave"

Answers "Then let's savor what we can of these fleeting moments
In a world that is about to pass us by, when are we gonna meet?
You know, in their awkward dance of passion, all people cry out for each other
Even those perfect arrangements of kindred spirits
Can end up in their own small nightmares
Life's one big juggling act but we don't do well alone.
My ghost is still visible
I've already planned out my burial at sea."

"Who am I?" collage (detail)

"The Armor of Despair"

mixed media
construction

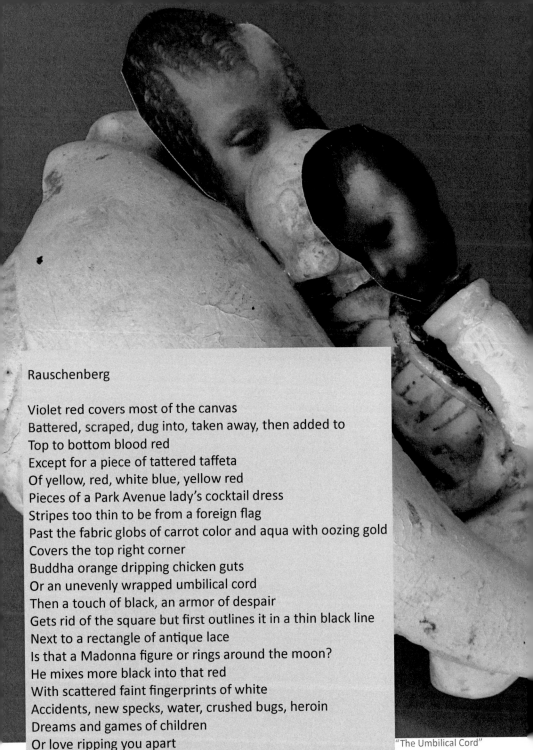

Rauschenberg

Violet red covers most of the canvas
Battered, scraped, dug into, taken away, then added to
Top to bottom blood red
Except for a piece of tattered taffeta
Of yellow, red, white blue, yellow red
Pieces of a Park Avenue lady's cocktail dress
Stripes too thin to be from a foreign flag
Past the fabric globs of carrot color and aqua with oozing gold
Covers the top right corner
Buddha orange dripping chicken guts
Or an unevenly wrapped umbilical cord
Then a touch of black, an armor of despair
Gets rid of the square but first outlines it in a thin black line
Next to a rectangle of antique lace
Is that a Madonna figure or rings around the moon?
He mixes more black into that red
With scattered faint fingerprints of white
Accidents, new specks, water, crushed bugs, heroin
Dreams and games of children
Or love ripping you apart
In the end, he throws from afar
Onto the canvas dripping to the floor
What's left of that can of violet red

"The Umbilical Cord"
mixed media
construction

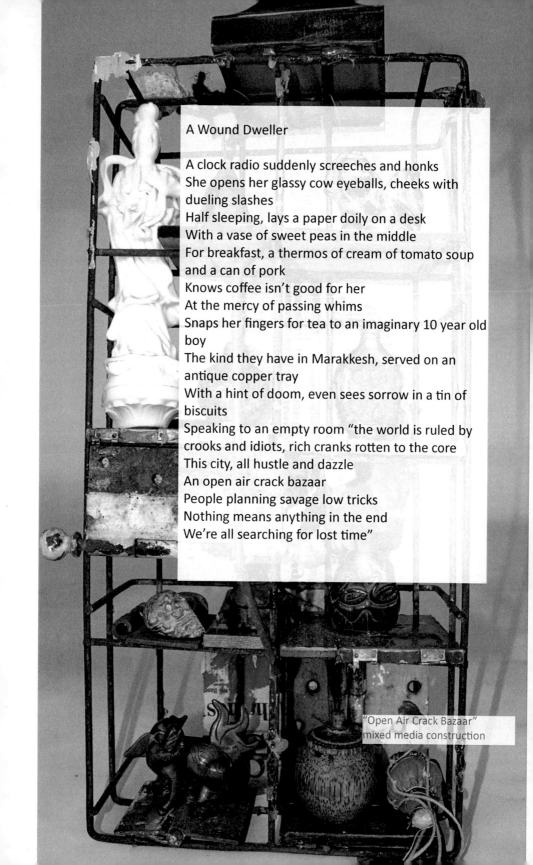

A Wound Dweller

A clock radio suddenly screeches and honks
She opens her glassy cow eyeballs, cheeks with
dueling slashes
Half sleeping, lays a paper doily on a desk
With a vase of sweet peas in the middle
For breakfast, a thermos of cream of tomato soup
and a can of pork
Knows coffee isn't good for her
At the mercy of passing whims
Snaps her fingers for tea to an imaginary 10 year old
boy
The kind they have in Marakkesh, served on an
antique copper tray
With a hint of doom, even sees sorrow in a tin of
biscuits
Speaking to an empty room "the world is ruled by
crooks and idiots, rich cranks rotten to the core
This city, all hustle and dazzle
An open air crack bazaar
People planning savage low tricks
Nothing means anything in the end
We're all searching for lost time"

"Open Air Crack Bazaar"
mixed media construction

At fourteen, she experienced a vision of the
Virgin Mary
Since then her past never went away
That constant sense of sickening dread.
A gift for lyricism when no one is looking
She dances round and round, shimmies and
shakes
Following her shadows in darkened rooms
For exercise, does laps without a pool

In her safe bed, down cushions and blankets
Watches horror films and riots on TV
Last night saw a blindfolded Sunni fanatic
Hung with shackled wrists then attacked by
rabid dogs
A screaming ISIS warrior
Or was it an al- Qaeda terrorist
Can't tell the difference
Her favorite film, The Hurt Locker
Likes that New Age loopiness
And living with a wild God
"All that is solid melts into air"
The terror never lets up

"Living With A Wild God"   collage (detail)

"Dreams and Games of Children" mixed media box

Where is my safe place?

Coming from a place of silence
I've always felt things in a solitary way
Like walking off a cliff as your body falls down to the gorge below
Or pushed through the eye of a needle, into a vanilla world
Imagine walking on green jello in a dress of puffballs and feathered
slippers
Those dreams and games of children
That state of wonder finding a hidden door from which they can see
The monster in the closet, the princess on the glass mount
A gold painted tooth fairy as beautiful as a bride
Cat's feet creeping by a flock of starving crows,
Little church ladies, touched by the spirits
Wearing a corsage of candy charms
Those hungry hearts, the secrets of the night

When I was a child
I used to pick out a cloud whirling around in space
It was where I wanted to live
Or on a wave that goes one into another

The house that I lived in was never a safe place
An oasis of horror in a desert of murderous nomads
No locks on the door, always listening for the knob to turn
The father invasion is like battling a ferocious lion
I just couldn't follow the path he wanted, the obvious
Searching instead for the unexpected, my own voice
A blast of faith blossoming into hope
Wanting to connect with something larger than this immediate life
Would I sooner come back a butterfly or a scorpion
Collapsing into a pile of mirrors while falling into a love trap
In my silence I still ask where is my safe place
Will the wolf always be knocking on my palace door?

"Where is My Safe Place?" mixed media box

"A Blast of Faith" mixed media box

Bloody Sunday

On the far side of the 60's
Vietnam
An ashen lunar landscape
Fragments stored against the ruins
Embedded despair
Glaring at a singed poster
Of a tin pot emperor, the immortal enemy
A pregnant woman goes into labor
As napalm bombs fall and splatter her body with flaming gel
Human sacrifice, bloody Sunday
At five thousand feet you can still smell the flesh burning
Descending into madness
People crying out for each other

Choking with human ash in this bombed out city
Ponds vaporize and canals boil
Bowing to the inevitable,
fleeing people combust as they run
Birds of prey, the madness of the macabre
It would have been better to take a cyanide capsule

Embers of war everywhere, under a big black sun
Is another child is brought into a burning world from a dead
mother?
Her sister holds the bloody mass in her trembling hands
Silently seething, the wretched of the earth
When millions of people are suffering
It becomes everyone's business
Vietnam

Flower children, psychedelic flashes
Drug addiction tailspins
Dying of a heroin overdose
Dark pleasure or dark pain?
You look into a mirror and see the face of a corpse
Opposing shadows exist, like a ghost on a glass negative
A dead utopia
Don't look now but the Flower Children are gone
When civilization falls, does it make a sound?

"The Wretched of the Earth"
mixed media box (detail)

"Embedded Despair"
mixed media box (detail)

73

Sorting Out Truth

At the World Trade Center
Motionless against the winter shining, white ashes and debris
In a smog-stained sky, in an open grave
There lies a perfect miniature Royal Crown bottle
Empty without so much as a scratch or scar
Who needed this for their next job interview
To tell their boss it ain't fair, get through another day
Of filing, copying, typing those endless briefs
Those lonely struggles.
Did someone lose half a mil in the market today
All of their mother-in-law's money, that saint in a stolen picture
In a moment of calm, checks his Rolex watch, reads his credit card slip
with twin $35 lobster claws, combs his toupee
Such bravado

Under a grid of black wire
A battered water park silently simmering
A litany of errors, the unspeakable
Heresy and treachery
Rambling back through dark passages
Buried secrets that will never be told
A half burnt box of a wedding dress in white
Weeks later she dies in black
Gestures of revolt, crazy is happening
The winds of war are blowing our way too
With the prospect of more loss.
We're bearing witness to the unspeakable
I find a child's Pac Man machine
The ghost lights of a long goodbye
How do the dead dream

"A Litany of Errors"   mixed media construction

"Life's Atrocities" mixed media box

To me life's atrocities are still happening
Going on right now everywhere in the world
Islam turning in on itself, ISIS Strongholds in Iraq, Syria
Burning down villages, tribal warfare,
Turn-away pictures of be-headings
Flooding in Bangladesh, chronic famine in Africa,
Ebola in Sierra Leone.
And us, in our chatty carloads of misfits and eating disorders
Arguing, should we stop at Roy Rogers, or Dunkin Donuts
Heinz ketchup or barbecue sauce
Why can't we make the choice

As we look at scattered newspaper pictures
A tour de force of mysterious dangers
People in fetal crouching postures
Wailing and dissolving, atrocities hardly being noticed
A destroyed bridge to a distant world
Yet we live with the consequences
The decisions of our elected leaders
And their oppressive dictators

Are there any more two-gulp bottles
Buried beneath this cemetery of scattered body parts,
DNA, guts and dreams
In this shimmering world of blind faith
How can you be a good person in a bad place
Three thousand ain't six million Holocaust deaths or
twenty-two thousand Bosnians, victims of ethnic cleansing
But it happened here, right here
In the wilderness of our city
That's why we will never forget

"Embedded Despair"
mixed media box

The World Needs a Hero

I remember newspaper clippings of Cambodia genocides
I saved the pictures
Standing against a crumbling wall under a green lemon sky
A line of young peasant soldiers
How helpless they were as they heard sounds of grief
Like a howl in a closet, the death rattle
Then a single bullet to the brain -- the world blotted out
Love, guts, gore everywhere
A greenish spit foams out of their mouths
Half tenderness, half horror, on what was once a face
Nearby another dead soldier lies alone on a deserted hill
Loaded down with decorations and glory
Tarnished medals and tattered red ribbons
Confining this young soldier to oblivion
We bow in a sacred time of mourning for all their global souls

Who are these dirty foot stamping blood thirsty people
Nostalgic for war
Suffocating in a moral swamp the dark part of our humanity
Those thousands of boys who fought as child soldiers
Now with arms and legs cut off
Begging for pennies in the market
A vast minstrel show
Find our dead warriors and take them home to their wailing widows
The world needs a hero

"Nostalgic For War"
mixed media box

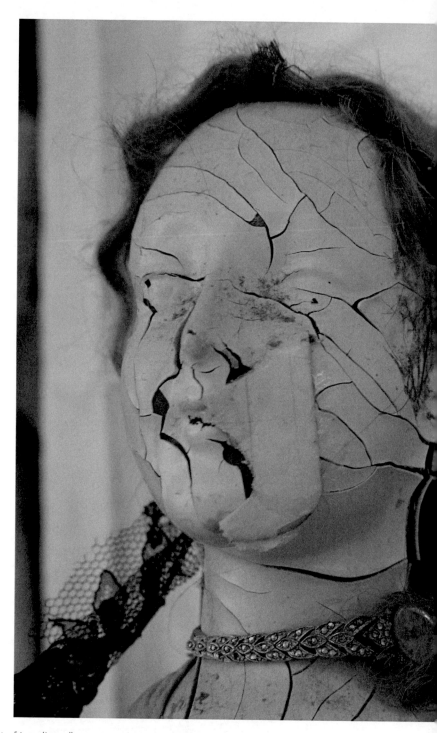

"The Weight of Loneliness" mixed media construction

There is Blood in the Water

On our million dollar block
My head deep into the pillow, I wake up exhausted,
The weight of loneliness pressing down on me.
Ass elevated by the other pillow
A cold wetness, he must've taken me from behind.
Surrounded by cigarette butts, unanswered letters
Unpaid bills, cups of half-drunk coffee.
Scattered and buried around the room
Clothes soiled with smudges and drippings
Even on my new black adored Armani.
My sketchbook of barren winter trees
On a striped Art Deco chair
Is tied with a tattered black ribbon
Doing all it can to hold the pages tightly together.

A scattered newspaper lays at the foot of my bed
The headlines: Kosovo, Ethnic Cleansing
Thousands of displaced refugees
With bodies looking like bugs smashed under glass.
It's like entering one's own nightmare
Those barbaric young people proudly carry big man guns
An inherited courage of ugliness
Unimagined slaughter, the worst of cruelty
Cannibalism, really.
Invested by their verminous, satanic charms
You can watch them sink into the morass of ignorance and brutality.
A reckless greed that will be inscribed in the fossil records
The survival of one's own blood and religion against all others.
Shame, the deeply buried force that drives them
Now waiting their turn to die for the homeland
As they eat their meals on corpses
Slaughterhouse Five.

In their burning thatched-roof villages
Shimmering on hot sands, packed like sardines
Watching people devour each other, vomiting into a ditch
Confusing the real with the unreal
Living in a world that has lost its memory.

The Invisible World   "Remembering and Forgetting" mixed media box(detail)

From the deepest dark brain cave
To the walls of his ego into the sea of oblivion
Remembering and forgetting
He sees inside of a dream, his life a throw of the dice
Bizarre. Grotesque. Beautiful.
His dream eyes see a Persian lamb coat
A cobblestone street in Odessa
A bed in steerage made of his mother's dowry
This joke of absurdity turns to bitter melancholy then visual bliss
Before his head hits the asphalt and breaks his skin
Looking as moronic as a skate rat punk who shoots a skinny black retriever
And sells its meat to a Chinese Restaurant.
Did you know that black dog is tastier than white?
Standing in the Castle of Eagles
He smells saturated tones of an African guillotine
Nine of ten colored girls undergoing genital cutting.

In our segregated narrow world
Nigger is still a sliming slur, an epithet
With our mean red-faced grit we are evil. Shitless. Shut off
Blindly upholding the old order.
Bigotry. Redemption. Transcendence.
 I too, am the displaced person
The one feeling orphaned by family
Pleading for deliverance from middle class utopia
Knowing we are all part of everything
Traveling without a map I left the main highway
For black smoke and a sliver of burning light
Wanting to be integrated, to be ripe, to go on
Then was stopped by the border police
A stranger coming into town

"Awash in Memories"   mixed media box

The Shadow that Cast Over My Life

My father read all of the Encyclopedia Britannica, A to Z
And the complete set of Mark Twain and Charles Dickens
While living in a house full of Chinese Buddha's
Made of amber, jade, lapis and milk glass memorabilia
The marriage effectively dead, his wife a Magdalene, untouchable, unlovable
A kind of Virgin Mary,
A victim of a disorienting emotional flu
Nightly eats a hoagie and falls in bed
With a bottle of Conquistador Tequila Dark and passes out
A ghost in the sunlight, awash in memories
He tells her I'll never be old" and secretly buys
Himself nine-hundred dollars' worth of Jean Paul Gaultier underwear
And light blue pink pure linen jackets.
"One day I'll be gone from your sizzling snake dance
Before you kill me with just a bite to the back of my neck

In your untamed nature, hips shivering like mine,
You huddle in my arms for warmth,
Fingernails stroking my underbelly.
Yet secretly hating me
I know I will be split off and abandoned by you
It's clearer than the ticks of a clock.
Mirror opposites, you know nothing about my private torment
Instead, I will die walking the rim of an active volcano, Mt. Erebus
Or have wild sex on a train to Adelaide
Maybe go to the sub-tropical shark filled waters of Galapagos
Diving under sea ice, coral with brilliant colors of tropical sea grass beds.
A glorious light will beckon me
I could go or stay, I choose the light
And you the devil, on a Catholic Sunday
A lawless woman on the run
A body without organs, a cave of forgotten dreams
Will leave my body in a dumpster
In this needy evil city of gorgeous soul sickness
You will use all my money chasing Flash Boys.
In a dover white asylum Shangri La
Instead of you, the shadow cast over my life
Will be a cemetery angel
Tear the dark veils off your eyes

"Cemetery Angel" mixed media construction

"I'll Never Be Old"   mixed media box

Memories in an Empty Room

From time to time
Childhood scars are rediscovered on my skin
It turns itself wrong side out
Like a sketch of a dream, a moth-eaten sweater
At the back of beyond
Collapsing under a shivering bird tree
And the endless sky, luminous and gray
I try to clear away dust and cobwebs of my life
A gorgeous messiness,
A smoke screen of small fates
A desperate longing to be anywhere but here
I am an incomplete magnum opus
Without a clue as to whom I used to be
I am nothing but desire and disaster, a flash voice
An illusion of the future

In a hospital ward I see reflections on an IV bag
Suspended between two beds
A mouth surrounded by tentacles
Buried in sunless depths of a hydrogen bomb
Or a hole from drilling deep into the coral reef?
And memories of people I have loved,
or wanted to love
Doesn't take much to get me started
flinching from flames
Watching the paint fleck from hotel walls,
A dog begging on two legs, looking like
an impatient lover
My dead dog Duncan
If you avoid memory you avoid life
You dishonor all the ghosts that created you
In my spiritual emptiness and confusion
I need to know what I am reinventing
The question is not what you look at
But what you see

"Like A Sketch of A Dream"
mixed media construction

84

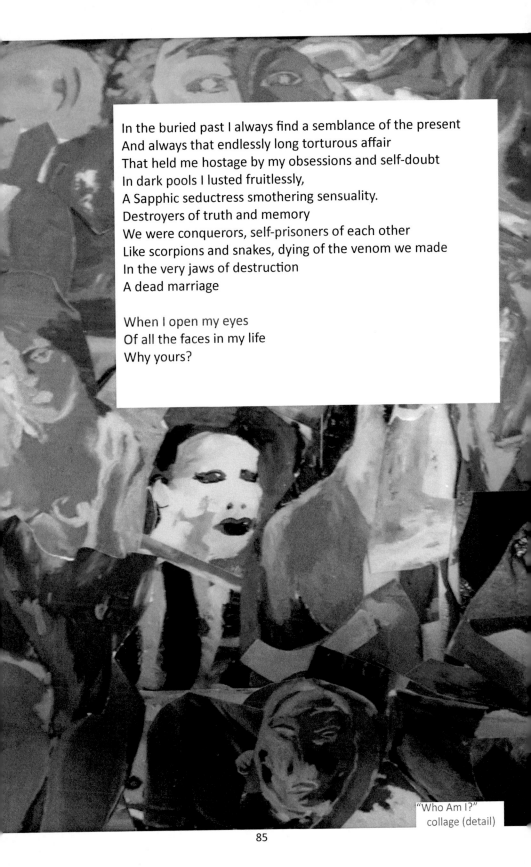

In the buried past I always find a semblance of the present
And always that endlessly long torturous affair
That held me hostage by my obsessions and self-doubt
In dark pools I lusted fruitlessly,
A Sapphic seductress smothering sensuality.
Destroyers of truth and memory
We were conquerors, self-prisoners of each other
Like scorpions and snakes, dying of the venom we made
In the very jaws of destruction
A dead marriage

When I open my eyes
Of all the faces in my life
Why yours?

"Who Am I?"
collage (detail)

"Silent Witness To My Life" mixed media box

River on Fire

Digging out from pest infested rooms, cockroaches and petite rats
Bedbugs by the millions on mildewed mattresses
Lay little white eggs that come out of their asses
Termites fall from the sink spigot
Fighting through dense spider webs
Home invaders try to come through roofs
Bats cling to busted houses, sagging in on themselves
Trees grow through the floors festooned with forest motifs
Picturesque devastation

Telephone books burn in the furnace for heat
Yet rusty pipes freeze and burst, banks repossess
The city smells of urine, dead fish and vomit
Buildings that don't have walls topple over, mingle with one another
Sounds of things coming apart
Like a deserted industrial Soviet town
Surrounded by rebels and thugs, even the clergy pack pistols
The new urban prairie
Behind every curtain an invisible man
A silent witness to my life

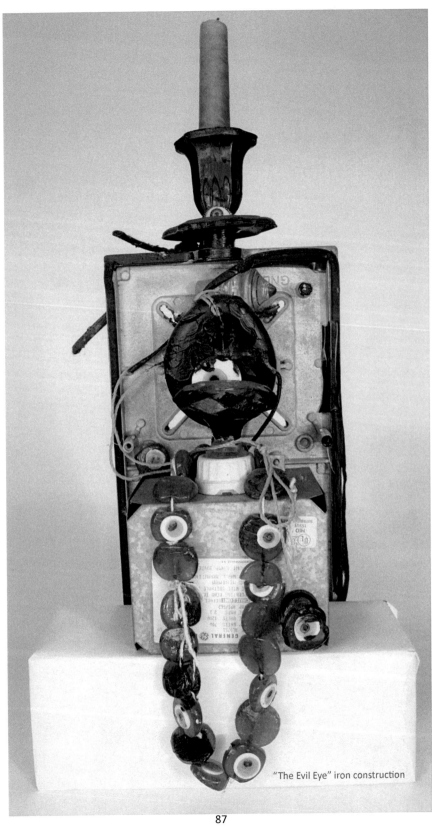

"The Evil Eye" iron construction

What is Rich?

To me, rich is eating organic mesclun
A field of greens, truffle puree and marrow reduction
Having collagen lips, liposuction
Sucking out useless fat from those inner thighs
Along with pulling out bulging varicose veins
And married to his Highness Sheikh Mohammad Bin Rafhid
Al Maktoun
Wearing Bulgari jewels with magenta four-ply silk
On glittering salmon skin from the Riviera sun
Sheer greed

A lifetime membership at the Meadows Club, Southampton
With its vacuumed grass tennis courts
And don't forget their strict dress code,
Even while viewing from the grandstands
"No bright colors please"
And I, all hustle and dazzle, spoiling their Eden
Distracting their players
Wearing purple red canary yellow culottes
The style of the day
With their Bigfoot Tactics, humiliated
I was asked to leave
With my scented trail of Jean Naté

"The Sense of An Ending"
mixed media construction
(detail)

The timelessness of Ascot races,
Hat of tulle horsehair netting tipped just so
Tea with the Queen
Me, the brief bright star of the moment
Surrounded by wealth, comfort, a sense of belonging

Then there is the old dowager from Greenwich, Connecticut
Grace Trowbridge, clever, crude and vulgar
Wears a dazzling stone necklace
Looking to me like good costume jewelry
"I love that chunky stuff you're wearing"
Stroking her two Siamese cats, Deeta and Erveé
Answers "My Dear, this is the world's greatest aquamarine"
She can barely crack a smirk
With a face of Restylane fillers
Her senile husband in formal wear
The descendant of a clown
Chases me round and round the dining room table
Until tripping on the handmade silk carpet
Imported years ago from Red China
No one sees this as "unusual"
Finally, the chauffeur hands me my bright cloth coat
Thanking him I say "did you know Orange is the new Black?"
Shriveling fast, their world is about to pass away
For me, I prefer a wild affair with Fabio DeLongi
Personal trainer to the stars

"No One Sees This As Unusual"
mixed media construction

"Mr. Brutus"
mixed media sculpture

The Tale of a Darkly Cynical Psychiatrist

He sits transfixed poring over satellite
images on Google Earth
A shrinking shell of a man,
Plagued with profound dysfunctional
secrets
His traumas came and stayed.
This glassy cow eyed Cold War Veteran,
with his rumbling stomach
Sits for hours in his favorite naugahyde
Eames chair
That gives him festering boils
on his buttocks
A King Emperor. A white knight riding to
the rescue of American paralysis.
His high level temper tantrums struggle for
pride and place.
A self-important windbag asks his patients
"And what does your ghost look like in the
sunlight?"
As he eats a Triple Whopper with mayo,
relish, sweet onions, cold fries drowning in
ketchup.
Closing his eyes, dreams of getting on Air
Force One, the Presidential helicopter
With access to the White House Tennis
Court as he gifts Obama his insights on
what it's like to be a black man in America.

When he sits on his throne there's a sound
of a poof pillow.
Then scatters cheap potpourri, disguising
the smell
Likes going native, his jacket antique safari
With deep pockets holding sourballs,
Bazooka gum, Brown Babies, Gummy
Bears, Jujubes.
Does this Buddha have genitals?

While writing his magnum opus he's coming to terms with the passing of time
Yet watches steaming scenes of lesbian porn
Imagining he still has the stamina of a Hercules, a Sisyphus.
Writing on the back of old faxes sick patient secrets, shifting fortunes,
The delicacy of family ties
Their prolonged traumas at the back of beyond
Captivating misery through a twisted Freudian screen
Toxic raindrops from a blackened cloud.

Mr. Brutus full of sexual innuendo
"Your boobs are sticking out"
He tells a patient who trades sex for powdered cocaine.
"You're a wound dweller merging the past with the present"
But among his own secrets
A bumper sticker plastered on the window of his 90's model Minicooper:
"Show me your tits." He has a gift for lyricism.
Ends the session with his typical words of wisdom
"We live in a zoo without cages, teeming with animal angels.
Dog and devil.
Spiritual emptiness, confusion located in the buried past. "
Then with a hint of doom
"There's a chicken outside your door that you're afraid will eat you.
The world of yesterday is over."

"The World of Yesterday is Over" mixed media box (detail)

"Katrina" mixed media box

Weather's Rage

A sudden violent storm turns the sky black
Then in flickering shadows torn metal screeching
Chimes at midnight, shutters banging endlessly
Electric wires snapping, shooting sparks
Lottie Leyna singing Kurt Wilde on a scratchy record
Arms outstretched, I can feel the earth moving
The dams overflow from the weather's rage
Turning itself the wrong side out
As a coastal promenade floats by this seaside destination
It becomes a salt lagoon, a bright turquoise stream.
A Shaman, bit of a mad man, a demon lover holds on to a canary
Carrying a small pet covered in a hot pink satin curtain
The powerful current smacks him in the face
A demon lover, déjà vu
I hear the hissing of an animal, a relentless squeeze
Like a Stag's roar for sex and violence.
The play of light and dark, earth and wings
As though the sky was lit by a thousand cigarettes
A glow in a dark painted room
No one knows the ending, Katrina

The outside world increasingly silent
Yet the air howls and sobs with laughter
Pushing against the darkness, a snarl of tangled cars
A hotel of white dreams
Clouds hang like soaked laundry nothing holding it together
As a curtain of rain blows across the lough
I tap on my neighbor's wall just to tell them I'm still alive
"Say hello to destruction and pain, say hello to everything"
I am as afraid as they are
The wolf that was outside me is inside me now
The boogey man is caught ringing my bell too.
Now a ghost in the house appears from an open door
A floating overstuffed closet with a rolled up rug
In camphor paper saved for better times
Awash in memories, possessions
Does it mean liberation, starting again, things you need to let go
But isn't there always some magic we can dance to
Some things must survive
And me, I'm in a small boat searching for land

"Some Things Must Survive" mixed media box

When the Clock Strikes Thirteen

Magic for me was my father pouring a colorless liquid
On the glass top of our kitchen table
Lighting a match, the liquid turned to flaming sky blue
The color of infinity, Antarctic blue
A rapid slide show of sky
It spread like fingers, branches of a tree
A steady stream of a river
The color of white smoke holding its footprint
A fat pan making fire crackers
Strange things were happening
The liquid like muted voices
Pencil figures, squids from outer space orbiting in the sky
The twist of a tail disappearing into a fog
As the clock strikes thirteen, a running Gazelle
A lone horseman in the distance vaporizes until it fades into nothingness
Where no life could go
That's when the light enters you
And you see a city of glass in a distorted mirror
Candles riddled with bugs
The sense of an ending, Paradise lost
 And I tell God I need to go home
But I am still the child of a Disney princess
Everyone must leave some kind of mark

"The Sense of An Ending"

mixed media construction

"Muted Voices" paper collage

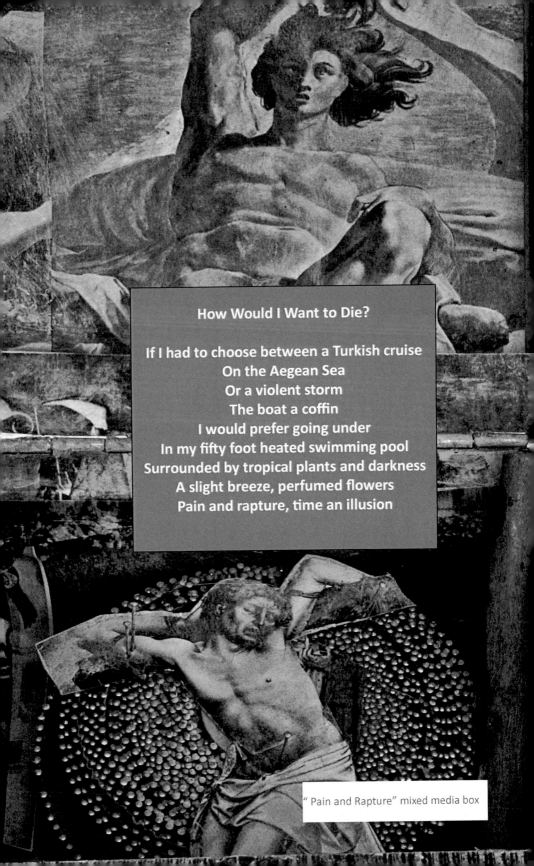

How Would I Want to Die?

If I had to choose between a Turkish cruise
On the Aegean Sea
Or a violent storm
The boat a coffin
I would prefer going under
In my fifty foot heated swimming pool
Surrounded by tropical plants and darkness
A slight breeze, perfumed flowers
Pain and rapture, time an illusion

" Pain and Rapture" mixed media box

"Families Past"
mixed media box

Voodoo Lady

In front of the Five and Dime
Sitting on cardboard boxes turned upside down
We would pick a negro lady, a cleaning girl
Sitting in mysterious shadows,
The color of her skin like soot from a forest fire
Some fat with legs spread apart, already wearing an apron
Some so thin their rolled stockings fell to their bedroom slippers
Do you think they were white inside?
My mother preferred the young ones
Three little pigs, this one just right
"I'll pay four dollars a day
If not enough, I'll choose someone else"
Walking the ten blocks home so slow
Clinging to her ragbag of torn up towels
The cleaning lady shuffled along like she had a club foot
Already sweating, smelled of cat piss and bleach
Canned peach shortcake
Then said with pride "I don't do windows."
She was a voodoo lady, could see right through you
Looked into your eyes, saw what you were really thinking
What you were really afraid of
Did she know my destiny
Or was she thinking of ghosts from families past?

You had to give her a sandwich, sometimes sliced steak
That looked gray ready for the garbage can
Or a thin spread of tuna fish on stale Tip-Top White Bread
Embarrassed, I knew there were better things in the fridge
It wasn't the right thing to do

Some people need to have gold stars
When she left, I gave her three from my private box
Because she worked so hard
Opened the window to get rid of her smell
And imagined the highest kite you could fly
Then dreamed of diving off a cliff, timing it to the waves
Surrounded by a hundred thousand doves
Or living in a treehouse, so high no one could ever touch or find me.

"So High No one Could Find Me"   mixed media box

"Voodoo Spirits"
construction with seed pods and found objects

This is For the War Effort

World War Two and the atom bomb
Frightening stories, images of devastation
In the New York Post
"What's doing, do you know the latest"
My father's voice trembling.
Old people save tin foil from cigarette packs
Until they were silver balls the size of your fists
The same with rubber bands
This for the war effort
Children stuff animals for European war orphans
Your fathers old socks with a button for the eye
You were made to feel guilty if you didn't eat every food morsel
Mothers said "Think of the starving refugees.
Remember you belong to the clean plate club""
Gifts of War Bonds for your birthday instead of frivolous toys
Seventeen fifty buys you twenty five dollars' worth by the time you're eighteen
Glorious victory gardens oozing with tomato plants we had never seen before

"There Must Be a Way Not to Die"
mixed media box

Air raid wardens rehearsed us for attack
"Turn off the lights, pull down the shades
Sit in the dark and wait for the all clear"
In school, portraits of Hitler, Hirohito, Mussolini
Buy a penny stamp to cover their faces so the enemy disappears
Uncle Sam pointing "I want you" And the poster "loose lips sink ships"
Families with a blue flag white star in the window
Meant "Our boy was sent to war, we wait".

Dream images
Soldiers with green tea ice cream skin
Dull yellow eyes streaked with blood
Crawling over dead bodies as if they were rocks
Finding their buddies with crushed rib cages popping, spleens
Cold dead fingers touching the Rosetta stone, grotesque gasps
Limbs hanging helplessly over rusty gates, the locks gone
Crossing enemy lines, their bloodied faces press into black grass
 So hungry and thirsty they eat cockroaches and drink cow piss
No longer a Nestlé's Chocolate Crush Nut bar in their pockets
Their destiny written in the stars
I remember reading a James Thurber poem
"Word War Two as everyone knows was the end of civilization
And all that was left was one man, one woman and one flower"
There must be a way not to die
It just hasn't been discovered yet

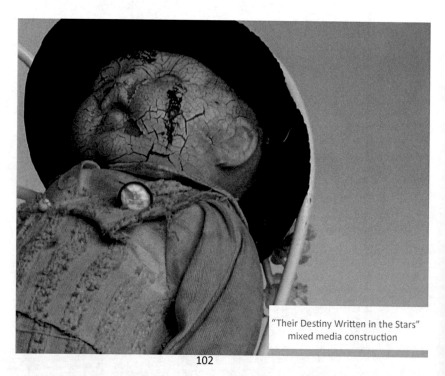

"Their Destiny Written in the Stars"
mixed media construction

" Once You See, You Cannot Unsee"
mixed media construction (detail)

House of Exile

In the glittering courts of Papal Rome
Similar to the Royal Palace of Persepolis or the
Macedonian Royal House
Sits a ghost on the throne, a warrior on horseback.
He scratches an inflamed tumor on his thigh that
seems life threatening,
Trying to find a comfortable position,
tossing and turning like an insomniac.
The Bishop.
Framed by lanky side curtains of hair, his lunar
moon face curls with revulsion
An Emperor disgusted by his spaghetti.
A fist guards his mouth, old lion eyes,
Has one foot in fascism, the other in mysticism.
Under a bright red skull cap, scorched and warped,
his fury strikes like a wave
His beady eyed gaze, daring the camera to take his
picture.
Now, leaning against a hallowed Doric column
His face reflects a constant sense of sickening dread
Knowing the comfortable day to day life could
disappear overnight
Haunted by the ghost of a defrocked priest.
Nearby, two marble coffins found in Fourth Century
tombs
Undisturbed, loaded with precious jewelry they say,
gold and silver vessels
A one-sided cardboard movie set.

Sounding like visceral glacial ice, spitting nonsense
Today's sermon
"The tiniest dream trickles into the ocean
Without these dreams there would be no ocean
Without the ocean there would be no shore
With no shore there is no place for our ghosts to
gather
Out of darkness you will come into the enlightened
present
At the cusp, once you see you cannot unsee."

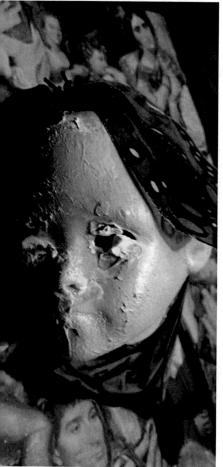

"No Place For Ghosts to Gather"
mixed media, collage (detail)

Bloody sacrifice!
Then crosses himself. Closed curtain.
This keeper of the flame's mission is to renew the purity of the tribe
Yet he wrings every dime possible from his devoted parish.

Hitting the trail, crossing the rainbow bridge in a black beetle gabardine suit.
Looking like a longtime coroner who could smother someone if the morphine didn't do the job.
To a sweet, newly-widowed parishioner, an amorous hand on a torrid breast.
Hell before breakfast. Sex with a sea creature.
Finally, the white hot iron of joy passes deliciously through his loins
Like the shock of pleasure from the blood of a slaughterhouse
Momentarily escapes himself.
Snorting beasts!
Lives in such a suspicious space, dreams often perverse
Seldom exuberant or romantic. Pitiless. Toxic.
His reflecting abstinence verges on black comedy.
It's biblical.

Without removing the cigar from his mouth
The dog, his best friend, watches him shave at night
Not to mention the three hours every morning doing his toilet.
He does share his spam and powdered milk or couscous for lunch.
Last night, dreamt he was shooting at a rat.
The rat turned out to be a boiled little girl
Served up with a fishtail attached to her body.

"Sex With A Sea Creature" mixed media box (detail)

105

II.

Below the gathering storm stands a crowd of aching hearts
Questing minds and fever dreams
Huddled in a worried corner
These wayward angels, faces of spiritual emptiness, confusion,
yet sometimes a crack of illumination in the armor of despair
With muted speech and simple-minded myths
They are doves of peace and flight, but their wings have been clipped
Their murmurs like rushing water of the footbaths they take
Before entering dimly lit catacombs of the great cathedral
To pray to their stillborn God, Saint Just
The simple duel between good and evil
We are all between the horror of death and love of spectacle
"God possesses the heavens but covets the earth"
People like me, the forty six million poor
What century is it outside?

"Wayward Angels" collage

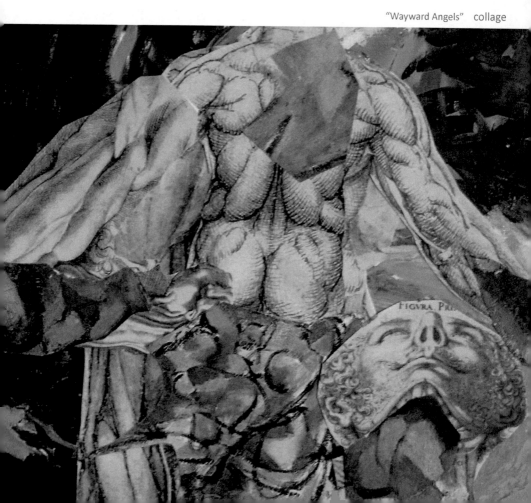

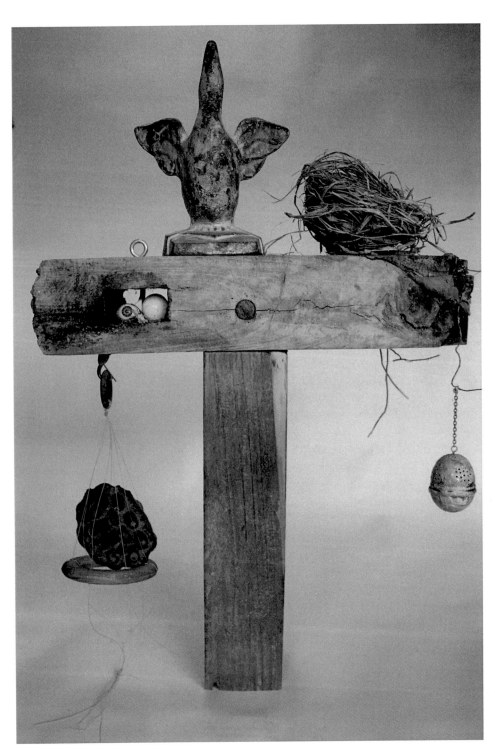

"What Century Is It Outside?" mixed media construction

Author's Artist Statement

My work is an exploration into the idea of space, the placement, proportion and power of objects, as well as the feelings they evoke. The basis of my work is autobiographic and built on fantasy, memory, and symbolism in the tradition of the Dada and Surrealist artists of the 1920s. I create boxed environments and assemblages featuring elements of surprise, unexpected juxtapositions while allowing my subconscious to express itself through the poetry embraced in the found, discarded and, often fragile object.

Being a collector and inspired by unique objects since my early childhood, I grew up in a period of history tainted by the devastation and deprivation of World War II. My passion for collecting was first inspired by my father, a clothing designer by trade, who struggled through the depression and the war years to support a family of five. We lived crammed into a one bedroom apartment in the Bronx. His extended family members were broken people, having been held captive in concentration camps, some used for human medical experiments. They spent their lives healing from the holocaust.

My father endured these years by building an immensely detailed four foot doll house, complete with fancy furnishings and decorative elements, with a clear glass protecting its open side. As a child I peered with a sense of longing into this fantasy world of many rooms, each preciously encapsulating a world beyond the one we could afford. Simple objects of beauty offered my father comfort and a sense of control. He surrounded us with a fortress of endless shelves of small Chinese sculptures - iconic and religious objects carved in lapis, jade and other precious stones- providing himself with moments of solace. At times he would hand me a cherished carving to touch, and at these moments I felt the transference of love and my closest connection to my father.

I have been greatly influenced by the work of the twentieth century constructivist, Joseph Cornell. I interpret his dreamlike glass-fronted shadow boxes as 'poetic theatres' filled with bric-a-brac and found objects. When I search for and select material for my own work, I respond emotionally to an object's past. I then work to transcend its identity to include multiple interpretations and force the viewer to see each component in a new light. I manipulate surfaces, deconstruct forms, lace together themes, and can wait a year or more for the ideal object to be discovered, resonate and subsequently, finished. Vastness. Isolation. Containment. Sacrifice. I search for the perfect articulation of feeling to describe a memory, an abstract idea - many times acting out a trauma from my past. Inspiration comes from also comes from the exotic environments, impressions,and colorful cultures I've experienced in my travels around the globe.

Building upon my career as an artist, set designer and hotel owner, I began to see rooms and space as big boxes. My rooms are filled with unique objects and the walls and tables are used to exhibit my assemblages. I now live in a large scale version of my father's original doll house, complete with white shingles, green shutters and the mahogany staircase. My spiritual life, my journeys, my environment and my art defines me.

photo by Richard Lewin

Made in the USA
Middletown, DE
21 November 2015